O IS FOR OYSTERCATCHER

A Book of Seaside ABCs

Barbara Patrizzi

DOWN
THE
SHORE
PUBLISHING

Harvey Cedars, New Jersey

Down The Shore Publishing Corp.
Box 3100, Harvey Cedars, NJ 08008
www.down-the-shore.com

The words "Down The Shore" and the Down The Shore Publishing logo
are a registered U.S. Trademark.

Printed in China
2 4 6 8 10 9 7 5 3 1
First Printing

Library of Congress Cataloging-in-Publication Data

Patrizzi, Barbara, 1959-

O is for oystercatcher : a book of seaside ABCs / Barbara Patrizzi.

p. cm

ISBN 1-59322-008-1

1. Coastal organisms. 2. Coastal organisms--Pictorial works. 3. English
language--Alphabet. I. Title

QH95.7.P38 2003

2003053171

For my grandfather, Carl Reiher,
and my friend Connie Jost.
I love and miss
you both.

Preface

For most of us, thoughts of the shore include images of lounging on a crowded beach or strolling on a bustling boardwalk. However, so much more awaits the curious explorer of our coastal regions. In a single day, one can visit vast areas of marsh and meadow, bay and bog, river and shoreline. Amidst the advance and retreat of the tides live an astounding variety of plant and animal life uniquely adapted to the wetlands — the ever-changing world between land and sea. In our coastal waters even more life forms abound.

We depend on coastal ecosystems for food, resources, protection from flooding and storms, and help with purification of our water supply. The coast needs our help, too. More than half of the wetlands in the U.S. have already been destroyed and our oceans are threatened by contamination. Only when we truly come to know and appreciate our coast, and the creatures and plants living there, will we garner the resources and the will to adequately restore and protect this vital part of our world.

We are never too young, or too old, to immerse ourselves in the natural world. This book can help on many levels to introduce children and adults alike to some of the fascinating species that inhabit the coast. Hopefully readers will be inspired to get out and get their feet wet, explore the rich and varied wildlife of our coastal regions, and try to make a difference.

Albacore

Speedy swimmer of the deep sea

This small species of tuna
is a champion swimmer.
Extremely agile and able to cover
long distances very quickly, albacore
can travel at speeds of over 50 miles
per hour. Although these fish inhabit
the open sea, albacore are also found
inshore around reefs and wrecks where they
feed on smaller fish. This tuna is popular
as a sport fish because of its tremendous power,
and also for its delicious flavor. Albacore is most
commonly sold in cans, but can also be found
at fresh fish markets.

Blue Crab

Fiesty underwater pirates that pinch

With eyes that extend out from their body on a stalk, blue crabs have nearly 360-degree vision and virtually no blind spot. Add fearless tenacity and startling speed to the mix, and you have a very successful bottom-dwelling predator. However, these scrappy creatures are just as likely to resort to scavenging and thievery to get a good meal. The blue crab is a real survivor, with an appetite for a wide variety of food, including vegetation, fish, snails, clams, and even other crabs. The blue crab is a valuable food source for humans; there are ongoing efforts to manage, conserve, and protect the crab population.

Cattails

Plants that are also known as punks!

These marsh plants provide protection and food to many marsh inhabitants. Birds perch in the long, blade-like leaves and also use them for nesting material. Muskrats gather the leaves for building their lodges. Fish seek protection around the underwater base of the cattails, while turtles eat the seeds and stems of the plants. Surprisingly, we humans also have many uses for cattails — in the manufacture of cornstarch, ethyl alcohol, burlap, and rayon. Native Americans also had a variety of uses for this interesting plant, including weaving baskets and mats out of the leaves, eating the starchy roots, and soaking the brown flower stalk in fat and using it as a torch.

Dolphin
The friendly mammal that loves to make waves!

Dolphins are curious, highly intelligent and friendly mammals that can be found in every one of the earth's oceans. Of the more than thirty species of dolphins, the bottlenose dolphin is the most familiar. Ocean aquariums keep bottlenose dolphins because of their adaptable and cooperative nature, but you can see them in the wild as well. These dolphins are very comfortable in shallow water, and can often be seen swimming in small pods along the coast.

Egret

Silent stalker of the marsh

In the summer egrets dot the green marsh like so many
tall white statues. Whether standing still or, in the case
of the snowy egret, shuffling their big yellow feet
to stir up prey, the graceful egret has perfect
aim when spearing fish in shallow water. During
breeding season, egrets are adorned with long
white plumes, which were prized in the early 1900s
for decorating hats and clothing. These ornamental
feathers were in such high demand that excessive
hunting brought the egret population to the brink
of extinction. Though efforts by conservationists
have greatly helped to increase their numbers,
wetland habitat destruction and coastal
development have prevented a complete recovery.

Fluke
Master of disguise, plus two funny eyes

Fluke, or summer flounder, are flat fish with both eyes on the top side of their bodies. Because of their unique shape, these fish look like magic carpets when they swim. However, fluke prefer to lie still on the ocean floor, or at the bottom of the bay, waiting for a meal to swim by. Fluke have a speckled and spotted appearance, which blends very well with the sandy bottom. This disguise makes it easy for the fish to ambush their prey. Fluke begin their lives looking like other fish, with their eyes on either side of their heads. As they mature, their bodies flatten and one eye migrates to join the other.

Green Turtle

A gentle green giant and long-distance swimmer

Largest of all hard-shelled sea turtles, adults commonly weigh over 300 pounds. When it is time to lay their eggs, the turtles swim as far as 600 miles from their foraging grounds and return to the same beaches where they were born. Nesting time is the only time the green turtles will come on land, and both adult and young are especially vulnerable to hunters and a variety of other predators. Hunted for its skin, meat, and shell, this beautiful and once common species is on the brink of extinction — today the green turtle is listed as threatened or endangered throughout its habitat. All sea turtles are protected today.

Horseshoe Crab

Is it a horseshoe? A crab? Guess again!

Horseshoe crabs have been around for a very long time, and haven't changed much in the last 360 million years. They are actually related to spiders and scorpions. Each spring, masses of horseshoe crabs emerge from the bay to spawn on bay beaches, where their eggs provide a crucial source of food for hungry, migrating shorebirds. This perfectly-timed meal makes a big difference in the survival of many bird species. Horseshoe crabs also play an important role in human medical testing. Their blood has unique properties which help detect drug impurities. The horseshoe crabs "donate" blood and then are returned to the sea. Because its numbers are in decline due to habitat loss and overharvesting, efforts are underway to protect this valuable species. Their largest nesting area is the Delaware Bay.

Irish Moss

Pretty and useful,
and seemingly everywhere

The branching layers of this seaweed
provide protection and
nutrition for all sorts of marine
life. Starfish, urchins, periwinkles,
seahorses, and microscopic
organisms are just some
of the life forms found in
and around clumps of Irish
moss. Interestingly, this
common saltwater plant
has many uses on land as well.
Also known as carrageen, Irish
moss serves as a thickening agent
in ice cream, toothpaste,
and cheese, and is used in the
manufacture of fertilizer and
industrial chemicals.

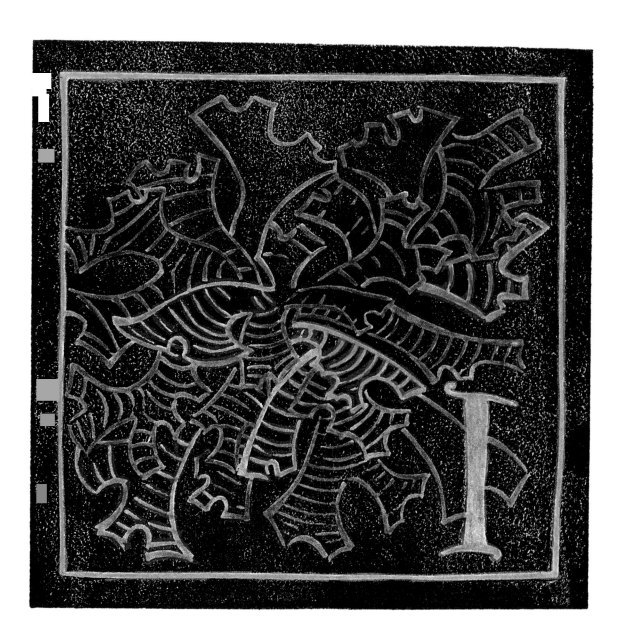

Jellyfish
Graceful and ghostly water dancers

Jellyfish are primitive organisms with no brain, heart, bones, or eyes. They have existed for over 650 million years. There are over 200 species found throughout the world. They gently pulse their way through the water, or are carried by wind, waves, and currents. People try to avoid them because of their ability to sting. When the jellyfish senses nearby movement, it fires off a stinging cell, called a nematocyst. This protects the jellyfish and helps it capture and subdue its prey. Most jellyfish are harmless to humans and are helpful in keeping ecosystems in balance. People benefit directly from jellyfish because of their use in the treatment of heart disease and certain types of cancer.

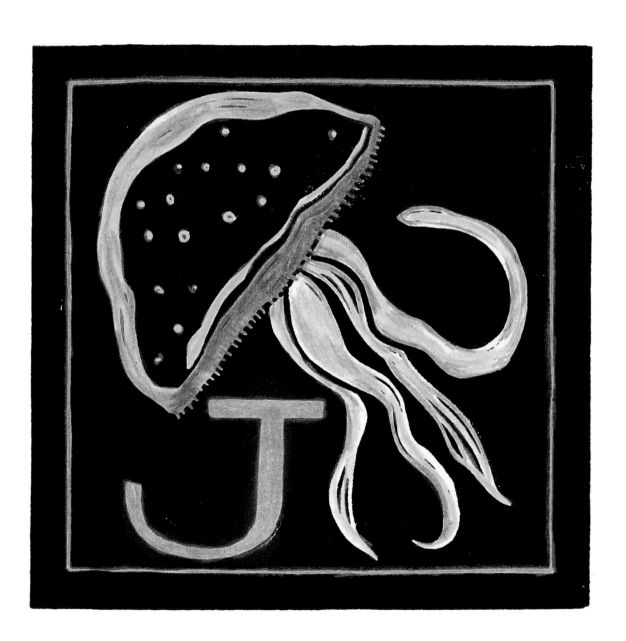

Kingfisher

The little-big bird that hovers and dives

Easily identifiable by its large head and beak, small body, and harsh, rattling cry, the belted kingfisher is often found patiently sitting on a favorite branch or piling overlooking the water. From this perch, he watches for small fish, crabs, and other prey. When movement is spotted, the kingfisher will take wing, hover briefly over the intended target, and then quickly plunge head first in the water to catch its prey. Found throughout Noarth America, these solitary birds are very territorial about their hunting grounds, and have specially adapted eyes for underwater vision!

Limpet

A tiny jewel that sticks close to home

Many different limpet species are found in the tidal zones of oceans all over the world. These tiny mollusks live in flattened conical shells. They attach themselves to rocks with their muscular foot. During the night, limpets travel several yards away from their home in search of algae to feed on (using a raspy, tongue-like organ called a radula) but they will then return to the same spot each day to rest. Limpets live in the exact same place for their entire life. The outer surface of the shell is rough, while the inner surface is smooth, shiny, and sometimes brightly colored.

Monarch

King of the insect airways

Unlike other butterfly species, monarchs cannot survive
long, cold winters. So, guided by the length of the day and
the temperature, North American monarchs can travel up to
three thousand miles on an incredible migratory journey to
Mexico. Each individual monarch will make the trip only once
during its lifetime. The migratory paths are the same each year,
and two major paths run along our eastern and western coastlines.
During the course of their journey, they always roost communily
and fly in masses. Monarchs choose traditional resting spots along
the way, where they will roost and feed on the nectar of flowering
seasonal plants, such as seaside goldenrod. Human admirers, attracted
by the quiet and colorful spectacle, stop to watch and photograph the
long-distance flyers. Fall is the best time to observe this
amazing undertaking.

Northern Diamondback Terrapin

A vulnerable diamond in the marsh

Of all the species of turtles in the world, only the northern diamondback terrapin is exclusively adapted to the coastal salt marsh. The terrapin is an agile and alert swimmer, and can live for 25 to 40 years, feeding on clams, snails, mussels, and fiddler crabs. In the late 1800s and early 1900s, terrapins were hunted nearly to extinction. This fact, along with the loss of wetland habitat, places the terrapin among the most threatened of all coastal animals. They also face a host of other dangers; many are hit by cars on their way to find a sandy spot to lay their eggs, and thousands more drown in commercial crab pots. Conservationists are launching intensive and creative efforts to reverse the decline in terrapin populations, such as requiring turtle excluders on crab pots. However, more needs to be done to save this beautiful and vulnerable species.

Oystercatcher

A boldly patterned shell-seeker

The oystercatcher gets its name from its favorite food, the oyster. It uses its large bill as a tool to pry open these and other bivalves. Oystercatcher chicks are able to see, walk, and feed themselves within hours of hatching from their eggs. This self-sufficiency is just one example of how resilient these maritime birds are. Unlike many coastal animals, the oystercatcher has been able to adapt and flourish in a wider and wider range. Once found only in isolated areas of the southern Atlantic coast, oystercatchers are now found as far north as Maine. This wading bird is easy to identify along the shoreline, jetties, and tidal mud flats. Look for its long, bright orange bill, and listen for the loud "KLEEP" of its piping call.

Pitch Pine

Scruffy survivor in a land of salt and sand

With its rough, scaly bark and scruffy crown of branches, the pitch pine is not the prettiest of trees. However, it is able to thrive along the coast where sandy soil, high winds, salt spray, and other environmental stress make survival difficult for most species of trees. The pitch pine has a refreshing scent, due in part to a very high resin content. Colonists used the resin to make tar and turpentine. In the winter months when other trees have lost their leaves, evergreens like the pitch pine provide birds and tree-dwelling mammals with much-needed protection from the season's harsh weather.

Quahog

A clam by any other name

Quahogs are large, hard-shelled clams. Native Americans carved and polished the white and purple shells to make a type of currency called wampum, and the name "quahog" is derived from the Narragansett word *poquaûhock*. Quahogs are commercially harvested (either raked or dredged) and classified by size: seed, bean, button, littleneck, topneck, cherrystone, and chowder. People eat clams in a variety of forms, including raw (cherrystones) or in chowders (chowder). All clams are bivalve mollusks, meaning that they are soft bodied animals (without a backbone) that live within two symmetrical shells.

Raptors
Soaring, sharp-eyed birds of prey

With eyesight many times more powerful than a human's, and a wide wingspan to hold them aloft on the wind, the northern harrier (marsh hawk), osprey, and bald eagle are all highly effective coastal predators known as raptors. Marsh hawks prefer a diet of small rodents, but will eat whatever prey is easily accessible, while osprey and bald eagles prefer fish. Gliding low over the salt marsh in search of meadow voles, the marsh hawk is one of the most commonly seen raptors. Bald eagles can be seen soaring high in slow, wide circles while they search for their prey, and the osprey's nest is usually the most obvious signs of their presence. These majestic birds were affected by the use of DDT and many became endangered species. Thanks to intense conservation efforts they have made a remarkable recovery.

Seahorse

The fish that eats like a horse

The seahorse is a fascinating animal with many unusual features. It has no stomach, digests its food inefficiently, and must therefore eat vast amounts of food — up to 250 small shrimp hourly. Although the seahorse is a fish, it is not protected by scales, but a series of jointed, bony plates and rings. This fish swims in a unique upright position, and although this swimming style is slow, it is very well suited to a life spent slipping quietly through dense vegetation. The seahorse's prehensile tail is also of great use in a habitat of thick sea grasses. It can be used to hitch a ride on a floating leaf of seaweed, or to hold onto rooted grasses and hide from predators. The male seahorses have brood pouches in which the female deposits eggs. The babies hatch and grow in the pouch, until they are ready to be born and are expelled into the sea.

Tautog

Easy does it for this swimmer

The tautog, or blackfish, has a large compressed body, made to move slowly and steadily around rock piles, wrecks, and reefs. Unlike fast swimmers, such as the albacore, which moves quickly and constantly through the open water, the tautog is relatively inactive. It conserves energy for catching prey or eluding danger, when quick bursts of speed are most needed. With its conical teeth and large, fleshy mouth, the tautog dines on small crusta-ceans. This popular sport fish can live for over 30 years, and can reach three feet in length.

Univalve

Its shell is its castle, on land and sea

Mollusks living in shells composed of one spiraling
piece are called univalves. There are many types of
univalves living on land, as well as in our seas and
inland waters. The whelk is one of the largest
univalves. In the summer, tiny whelks develop
inside strings of white, octagonal egg cases.
Many whelks will emerge from each egg case
in miniature, fully formed shells. Univalves
have calcium-rich blood, and as the tiny
animals mature, some of the calcium
separates from the body to form thin
layers of the strong, protective
shell. Univalves are important
food sources for animals
and humans
alike.

Virginia Opossum

This prowler keeps its babies in tow

There are many nocturnal mammals inhabiting the coast who are not easily observed during the day. One of these is the Virginia Opossum, North America's only native marsupial. The female opossum has a pouch where newborn babies will develop and be nourished for about two months. Although the opossum is a primitive animal with a relatively small brain, its extreme adaptability compensates somewhat for its lack of intelligence. Able to live in many environments, the opossum will make its den in any sheltered area, and will move frequently if necessary. It is a good climber, with dexterous paws and a prehensile tail. A wide variety of foods will satisfy this omnivore, from plants and worms to frogs and birds. The adaptable nature of the opossum makes it well suited to life along the coast.

White Ibis

Birds of a feather that really flock together

These long-legged birds are commonly seen in large colonies, and are found along the Gulf and southern Atlantic coast. White ibis nest in flocks, and are often seen roosting in masses on the limbs of closely grouped trees. Colonies of over 60,000 birds have been reported. Slowly wading in the shallows of estuaries, lagoons, and marshes, white ibis probe for fish, frogs, crustaceans, and insects with their long, curved bills. It is wonderful to see these birds in flight, flapping and gliding across the sky with their long necks outstretched. Another common member of the ibis family is the glossy ibis. It has similar habits; however, its purplish, glossy feathers appear black, and it ranges along the Atlantic coast as far north as Maine.

Zygoptera
Damsels and dragons that do more than fly

Commonly known as the damselfly, this insect begins life underwater, breathing through gills. As an adult, the damselfly takes wing. It has the ability to perform all sorts of aerial stunts; including rapid directional change, backwards and sideways flight, drops and dodges, quick stops and more. This powerful and talented flyer can reach speeds of up to 30 miles per hour, and possesses excellent vision. Smaller flying insects have little chance to escape this agile predator, who uses bristled legs to scoop its prey out of midair. The dragonfly is a close relative of the damselfly, but they can be easily distinguished: The dragonfly holds its wings horizontally while at rest; the damselfly holds them vertically. Both types of insects have existed for at least 300 million years.

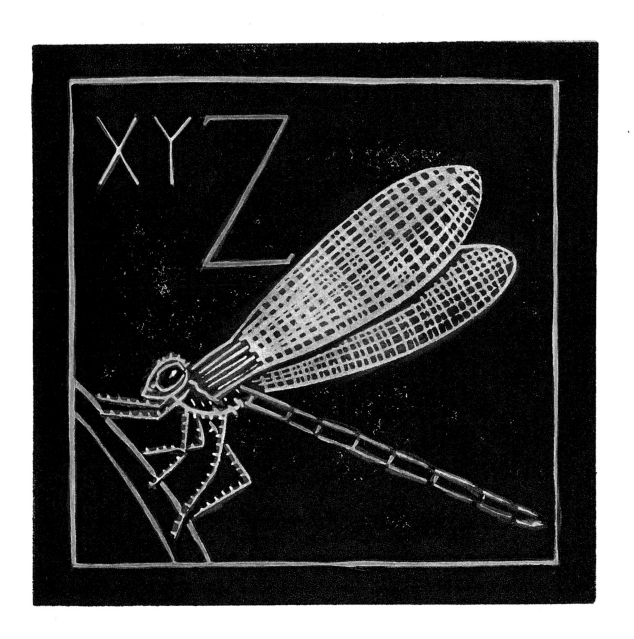

acknowledgments

This book would not have been possible without the talent and dedication of Leslee Ganss and Ray Fisk at Down The Shore Publishing. Thanks also to Marilyn Keating for her friendship and technical assistance, Tina Nolan for her love, encouragement and life-sustaining culinary support, and lastly, to my parents, Joseph and Jacqueline Patrizzi for their infinite love and generosity.

about the artwork

Relief printmaking is probably the oldest of all printmaking techniques. Each image in this book is a relief print made from a linoleum block (oxidized linseed oil, resin and cork dust on a Hessian support). Very simply, a design is carved into the surface of the linoleum with sharp metal tools, ink is applied to the raised remaining areas and paper is then pressed against the inked surface. The black part of the resulting image was the raised (inked) area on the block. The remaining white areas on the print were then hand-colored using polychrome pencils.

about the artist

Barbara Patrizzi grew up in southern New Jersey. She received her BFA from University of the Arts (then Philadelphia College of Art) in Philadelphia, PA, in 1981. She has exhibited nationally, and her paintings and sculpture are held in private collections throughout the country.

She currently resides in Philadelphia and Somers Point, NJ, where she lives with her partner and various four-legged friends, and keeps busy swimming, kayaking and gardening. This is her first book.

Down The Shore Publishing offers other book and calendar
titles (with a special emphasis on the mid-Atlantic coast).
For a free catalog, or to be added to our mailing list,
just send us a request:

Down The Shore Publishing
P.O. Box 3100
Harvey Cedars, NJ 08008

www.down-the-shore.com